JN418757

TOP LEVEL WRITING SENSE THE ONE I

For Elite Group

TOP LEVEL **WRITING** SENSE
THE ONE
For Elite Group

초판 1쇄 발행 2007년 8월 28일

지은이 한일
펴낸이 신성현 • 오상욱
만든이 홍수인 • 박진아
펴낸곳 도서출판 아이엠북스
121-884 서울시 마포구 연남동 567-39 302호
Tel. 02)3141-9508 Fax. 02)3141-9504
북디자인 A&A 에이앤에이 디자인
Tel. 02)2285-2022 Fax. 02)2285-2023
출판등록 2006년 6월 7일 제 313-2006-000122호
ISBN 978-89-92334-29-7 14740

www.iambooks.co.kr

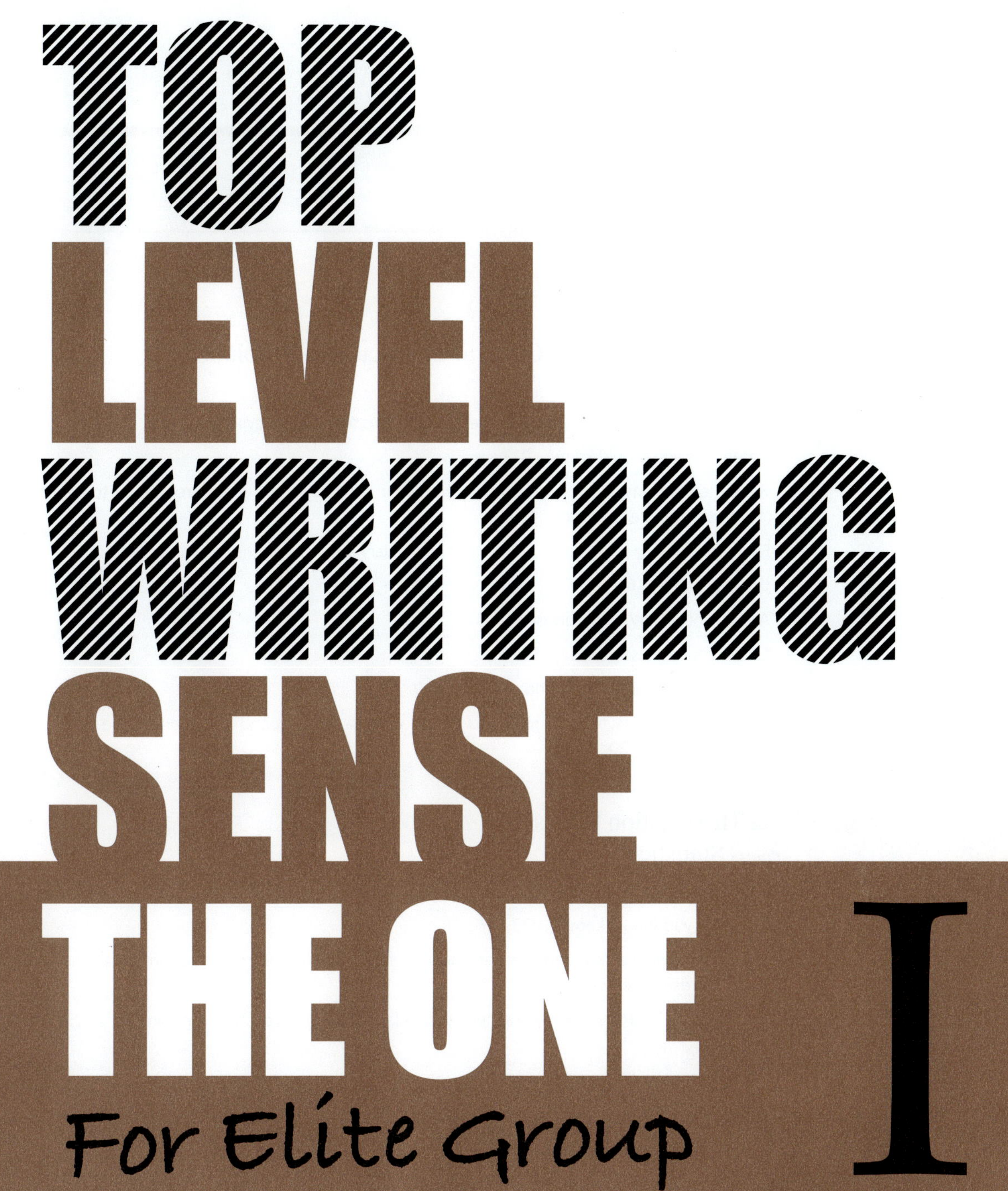

Written by **IL HAN**

I am books

Contents

Composition & Character

The purpose of this practice is to have you experience the high level of writing and ready for the studying in a higher educational institution.

The listed vocabulary follows the sequence of the content, not randomly mixed. This will help you find the appropriate vocabulary for your writing. Vocabulary here is not only helpful for the given writing but also leading you to the place where you are to be intelligent and educated.

This is one of the translations for the given material. It is worth noting that many expressions used here are the professional level. Since you are assumed to write it in your own level, you should not blame yourself when you see differences between your writing and this article.

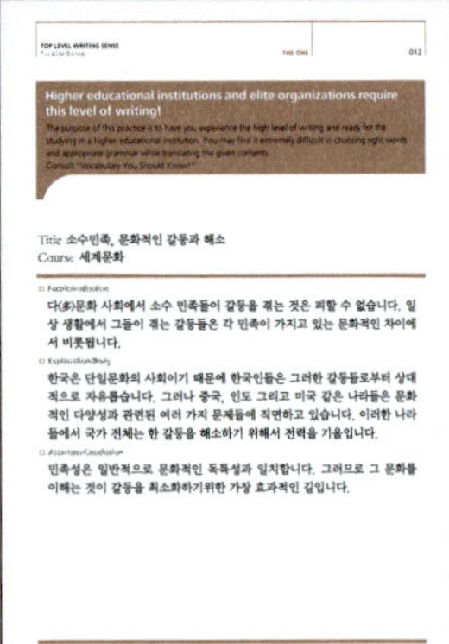

Higher educational institutions and elite organizations require this level of writing!

Title 소수민족, 문화적인 갈등과 해소
Course: 세계문화

다(多)문화 사회에서 소수 민족들이 갈등을 겪는 것은 피할 수 없습니다. 일상 생활에서 그들이 겪는 갈등들은 각 민족이 가지고 있는 문화적인 차이에서 비롯됩니다.

한국은 단일문화의 사회이기 때문에 한국인들은 그러한 갈등들로부터 상대적으로 자유롭습니다. 그러나 중국, 인도 그리고 미국 같은 나라들은 문화적인 다양성과 관련된 여러 가지 문제들에 직면하고 있습니다. 이러한 나라들에서 국가 전체는 한 갈등을 해소하기 위해서 전력을 기울입니다.

민족성은 일반적으로 문화적인 독특성과 일치합니다. 그러므로 그 문화를 이해는 것이 갈등을 최소화하기위한 가장 효과적인 길입니다.

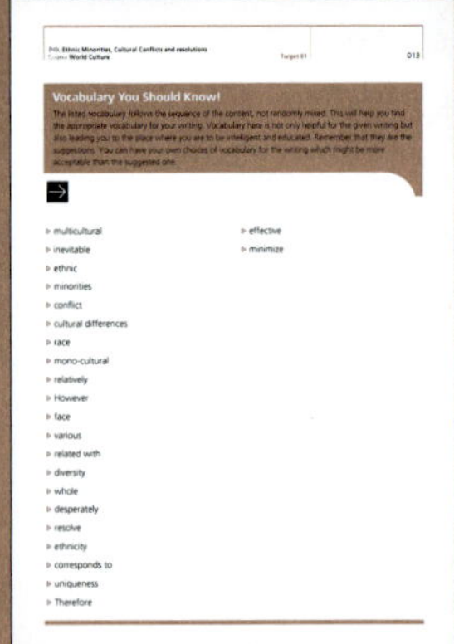

Vocabulary You Should Know!

- multicultural
- inevitable
- ethnic
- minorities
- conflict
- cultural differences
- race
- mono-cultural
- relatively
- However
- face
- various
- related with
- diversity
- whole
- desperately
- resolve
- ethnicity
- corresponds to
- uniqueness
- Therefore
- effective
- minimize

Read the following article and compare with your writing. As you read through, try to memorize the colored words and expressions.

Title Ethnic Minorities, Cultural Canflicts and resolutions
Course: World Culture

In a multicultural society, it is inevitable for the ethnic minorities to experience a conflict. Conflicts that they experience in their everyday life are coming from the cultural differences that each race has.

Since Korea is a mono-cultural society, Koreans are relatively free from such conflicts. However, such countries as China, India, and America face various problems related with the cultural diversity. In these countries, a whole nation fights desperately (devote its best efforts) to resolve one conflict.

Ethnicity generally corresponds to the cultural uniqueness. Therefore, understanding the culture is the most effective way to minimize the conflict.

Try to find easier vocabulary and expressions for the blank than you have written previously. You can see what is academic and what is casual. This practice enhances your memory of the words and its practicality. You can also have a clear understanding for the synonyms.

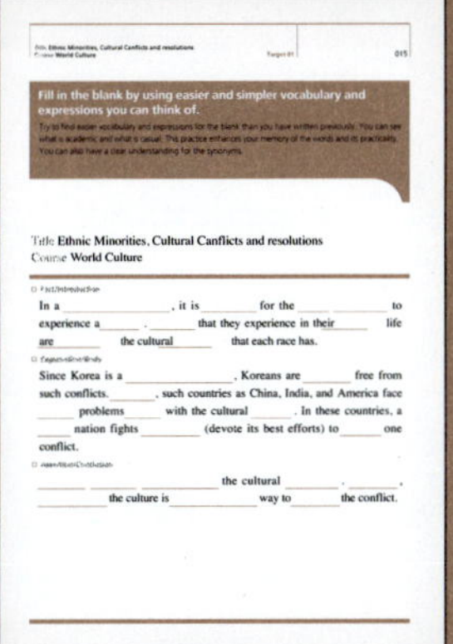

Compare the vocabulary and phrases here with those you have used previously.

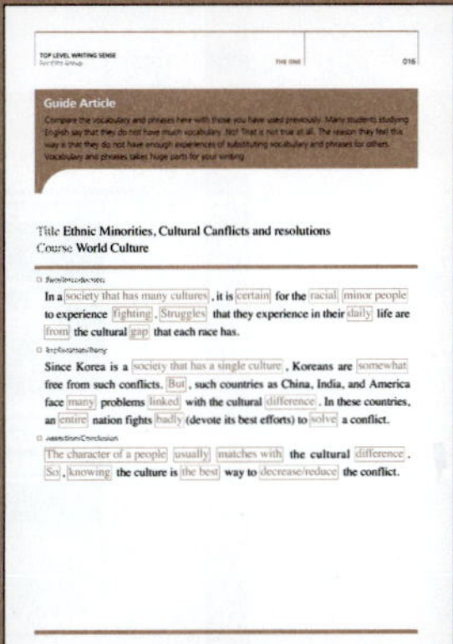

What can be used as a substitute of the word and phrase below? Feel free to refer to the previous article.

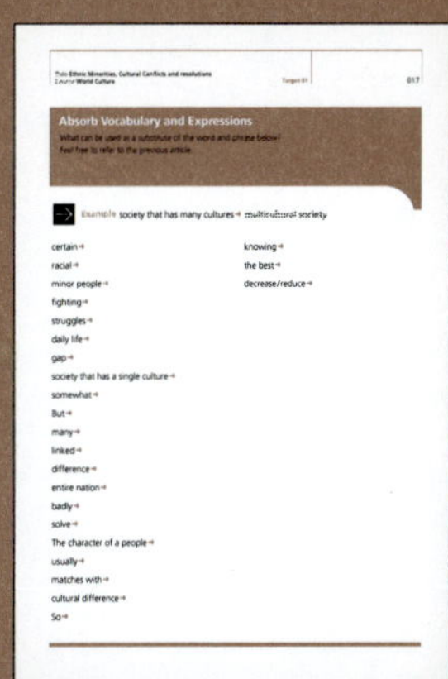

Composition & Character

Make a sentence that contains the given word and phrase. Use the given words for any parts of speech such as a subject, verb, object, preposition object etc.

Change the colored words and expressions to more difficult and academic ones! Knowing only one word for the writing will limit your skill, so you should have the alternatives. This practice will lead you to the state-of-art academic and formal writing.

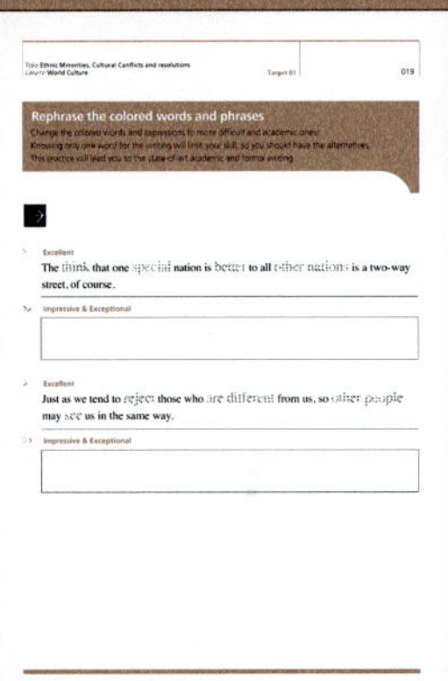
Rephrase the colored words and phrases

Excellent

The think that one special nation is better to all other nations is a two-way street, of course.

Impressive & Exceptional

Excellent

Just as we tend to reject those who are different from us, so other people may see us in the same way.

Impressive & Exceptional

You can find more reading materials in this website and expand your knowledge for the rapidly changing world.

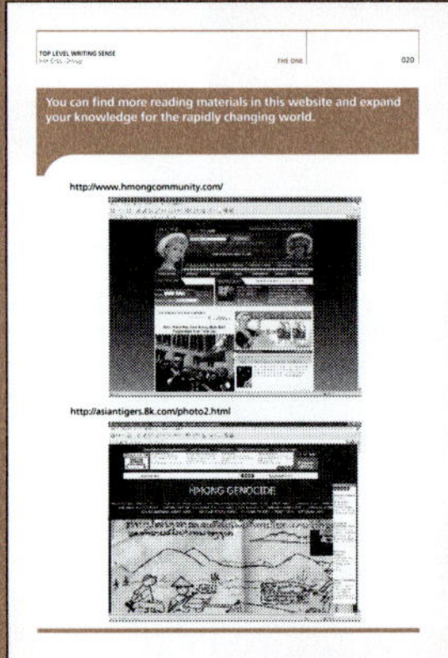
You can find more reading materials in this website and expand your knowledge for the rapidly changing world.

Guideline

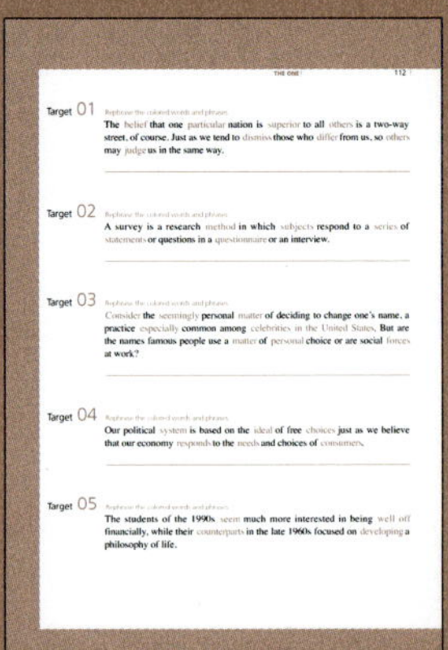

Level

Junior in University
TOEFL 6.0
1~1 and a half years of studying in English speaking countries

Approximate word counts

95 words

Required Skill

Words used for this writing "inevitable," "minorities," "mono-cultural," "diversity," "desperately," "resolve," "corresponds to," "minimize."

Target 01

Higher educational institutions and elite organizations require this level of writing!

The purpose of this practice is to have you experience the high level of writing and ready for the studying in a higher educational institution. You may find it extremely difficult in choosing right words and appropriate grammar while translating the given contents.
Consult "Vocabulary You Should Know!"

Title 소수민족, 문화적인 갈등과 해소
Course 세계문화

□ Fact/Introduction

다(多)문화 사회에서 소수 민족들이 갈등을 겪는 것은 피할 수 없습니다. 일상 생활에서 그들이 겪는 갈등들은 각 민족이 가지고 있는 문화적인 차이에서 비롯됩니다.

□ Explanation/Body

한국은 단일문화의 사회이기 때문에 한국인들은 그러한 갈등들로부터 상대적으로 자유롭습니다. 그러나 중국, 인도 그리고 미국 같은 나라들은 문화적인 다양성과 관련된 여러 가지 문제들에 직면하고 있습니다. 이러한 나라들에서 국가 전체는 한 갈등을 해소하기 위해서 전력을 기울입니다.

□ Assertion/Conclusion

민족성은 일반적으로 문화적인 독특성과 일치합니다. 그러므로 그 문화를 이해는 것이 갈등을 최소화하기위한 가장 효과적인 길입니다.

Vocabulary You Should Know!

The listed vocabulary follows the sequence of the content, not randomly mixed. This will help you find the appropriate vocabulary for your writing. Vocabulary here is not only helpful for the given writing but also leading you to the place where you are to be intelligent and educated. Remember that they are the suggestions. You can have your own choices of vocabulary for the writing which might be more acceptable than the suggested one.

- ▷ multicultural
- ▷ inevitable
- ▷ ethnic
- ▷ minorities
- ▷ conflict
- ▷ cultural differences
- ▷ race
- ▷ mono-cultural
- ▷ relatively
- ▷ However
- ▷ face
- ▷ various
- ▷ related with
- ▷ diversity
- ▷ whole
- ▷ desperately
- ▷ resolve
- ▷ ethnicity
- ▷ corresponds to
- ▷ uniqueness
- ▷ Therefore
- ▷ effective
- ▷ minimize

Read the following article and compare with your writing. As you read through, try to memorize the colored words and expressions.

This is one of the translations for the given material. It is worth noting that many expressions used here are the professional level. Since you are assumed to write it in your own level, you should not blame yourself when you see differences between your writing and this article.

Title Ethnic Minorities, Cultural Conflicts and Resolutions
Course World Culture

□ **Fact/Introduction**

In a multicultural society, it is inevitable for the ethnic minorities to experience a conflict. Conflicts that they experience in their everyday life are coming from the cultural differences that each race has.

□ **Explanation/Body**

Since Korea is a mono-cultural society, Koreans are relatively free from such conflicts. However, such countries as China, India, and America face various problems related with the cultural diversity. In these countries, a whole nation fights desperately (devote its best efforts) to resolve one conflict.

□ **Assertion/Conclusion**

Ethnicity generally corresponds to the cultural uniqueness. Therefore, understanding the culture is the most effective way to minimize the conflict.

Fill in the blank by using easier and simpler vocabulary and expressions you can think of.

Try to find easier vocabulary and expressions for the blank than you have written previously. You can see what is academic and what is casual. This practice enhances your memory of the words and its practicality. You can also have a clear understanding for the synonyms.

Title Ethnic Minorities, Cultural Conflicts and Resolutions
Course World Culture

□ Fact/Introduction

In a ____________, it is ________ for the ______ ________ to experience a ______. ________ that they experience in their ________ life are ________ the cultural ________ that each race has.

□ Explanation/Body

Since Korea is a ____________, Koreans are ________ free from such conflicts. ________, such countries as China, India, and America face ______ problems ______ with the cultural ______. In these countries, a ______ nation fights ________ (devote its best efforts) to ______ one conflict.

□ Assertion/Conclusion

______ ______ __________ the cultural ________. ________, ________ the culture is __________ way to ________ the conflict.

Guide Article

Compare the vocabulary and phrases here with those you have used previously. Many students studying English say that they do not have much vocabulary. No! That is not true at all. The reason they feel this way is that they do not have enough experiences of substituting vocabulary and phrases for others. Vocabulary and phrases takes huge parts for your writing.

Title Ethnic Minorities, Cultural Conflicts and Resolutions
Course World Culture

□ Fact/Introduction

In a society that has many cultures, it is certain for the racial minor people to experience fighting. Struggles that they experience in their daily life are from the cultural gap that each race has.

□ Explanation/Body

Since Korea is a society that has a single culture, Koreans are somewhat free from such conflicts. But, such countries as China, India, and America face many problems linked with the cultural difference. In these countries, an entire nation fights badly(devote its best efforts) to solve a conflict.

□ Assertion/Conclusion

The character of a people usually matches with the cultural difference. So, knowing the culture is the best way to decrease/reduce the conflict.

Absorb Vocabulary and Expressions

What can be used as a substitute of the word and phrase below?
Feel free to refer to the previous article.

Example society that has many cultures → **multicultural society**

certain →

racial →

minor people →

fighting →

struggles →

daily life →

gap →

society that has a single culture →

somewhat →

But →

many →

linked →

difference →

entire nation →

badly →

solve →

The character of a people →

usually →

matches with →

cultural difference →

So →

knowing →

the best →

decrease/reduce →

Create Your Own Sentence

-Make a sentence that contains the given word and phrase.
-Use the given words for any parts of speech such as a subject, verb, object, preposition object etc.
-You can change the form of the words.

1 multicultural

▶

2 ethnic minorities

▶

3 mono-cultural

▶

4 related with

▶

5 diversity

▶

6. whole nation

▶

7 resolve

▶

8 ethnicity

▶

9 corresponds to

▶

10 minimize

▶

Rephrase the colored words and phrases

Change the colored words and expressions to more difficult and academic ones!
Knowing only one word for the writing will limit your skill, so you should have the alternatives.
This practice will lead you to the state-of-art academic and formal writing.

> Excellent

The think that one special nation is better to all other nations is a two-way street, of course.

>> Impressive & Exceptional

▶

> Excellent

Just as we tend to reject those who are different from us, so other people may see us in the same way.

>> Impressive & Exceptional

▶

You can find more reading materials in this website and expand your knowledge for the rapidly changing world.

http://www.hmongcommunity.com/

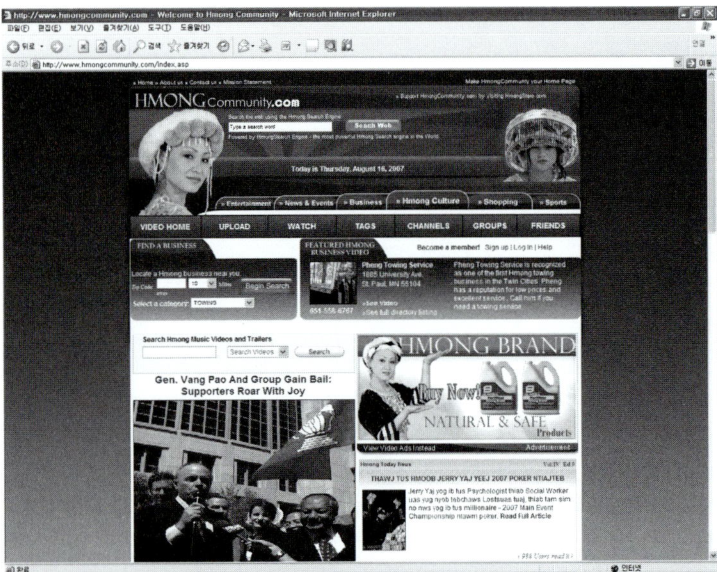

http://asiantigers.8k.com/photo2.html

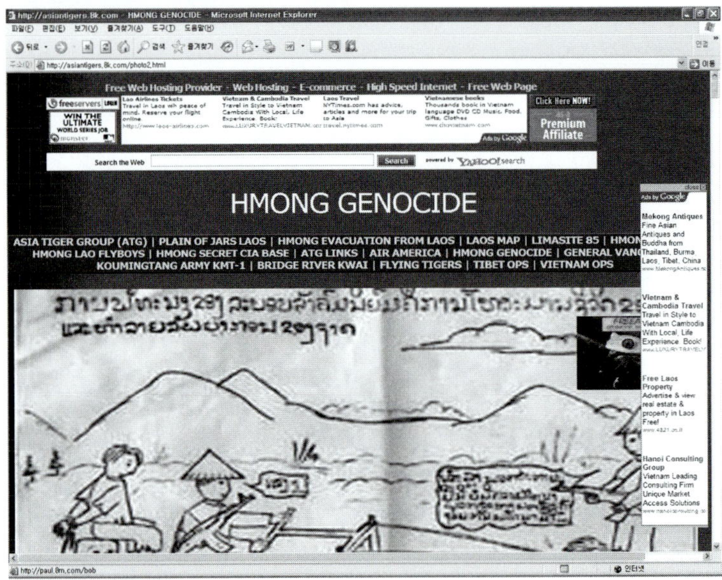

Level

Junior in University
TOEFL 6.0
2 years of studying in English speaking countries

Approximate word counts

96 words

Required Skill

Important academic words "be one step closer," "uncertain," "gather information," "standard procedure," "hypothesize," "conduct," "when necessary," "theorize," "keep in mind," "educated guess," "concrete," "to note," "vague," "solid," "surrounding," "context," "that is," "single."

Target 02

Higher educational institutions and elite organizations require this level of writing!

The purpose of this practice is to have you experience the high level of writing and ready for the studying in a higher educational institution. You may find it extremely difficult in choosing right words and appropriate grammar while translating the given contents.
Consult "Vocabulary You Should Know!"

Title 이론 구성 윤리
Course 통계학

□ Fact/Introduction

우리는 불확실한 질문에 한 발짝 더 가까이 다가가기 위해서 가능한 많은 정보를 모아야 합니다. 그 다음에, 가설을 세우고, 조사를 하고, 필요하면 수정을 하고, 그리고 이론을 세우는 정해진 순서를 따라야 합니다.

□ Explanation/Body

우리가 마음속에 기억해야 하는 것은 지적(知的)인 추측이라고 해서 항상 구체적인 해답을 보장하지는 않는다는 점입니다. 그러므로 우리는 모호한 해답일지라도 구체적인 해답처럼 똑같이 중요하게 취급해야 합니다.

□ Assertion/Conclusion

우리가 찾은 해답이 주변 상황이나 배경 정보에 따라서 변할 수 있다는 것을 유념(留念) 하는 것은 중요합니다; 즉, 불확실한 우리의 세상에서 하나 밖에 없는 구체적인 해답은 사실상 없다는 말입니다.

Vocabulary You Should Know!

The listed vocabulary follows the sequence of the content, not randomly mixed.This will help you find the appropriate vocabulary for your writing. Vocabulary here is not only helpful for the given writing but also leading you to the place where you are to be intelligent and educated. Remember that they are the suggestions. You can have your own choices of vocabulary for the writing which might be more acceptable than the suggested one.

- ▷ one step closer
- ▷ uncertain
- ▷ gather
- ▷ standard
- ▷ procedure
- ▷ hypothesize
- ▷ conduct
- ▷ revise
- ▷ theorize
- ▷ keep in mind
- ▷ educated guess
- ▷ guarantee
- ▷ concrete
- ▷ treat
- ▷ vague
- ▷ solid
- ▷ note
- ▷ according to
- ▷ context
- ▷ that is
- ▷ uncertainty

Read the following article and compare with your writing. As you read through, try to memorize the colored words and expressions.

This is one of the translations for the given material. It is worth noting that many expressions used here are the professional level. Since you are assumed to write it in your own level, you should not blame yourself when you see differences between your writing and this article.

Title Theorization Ethics
Course Statistics

□ **Fact/Introduction**

To be one step closer to the uncertain question, we should gather information as much as possible. Then, we should follow the standard procedure; hypothesize, conduct a research, revise when necessary, and theorize.

□ **Explanation/Body**

The point we should keep in mind is that an educated guess doesn't always guarantee a concrete answer. Therefore, we should treat even vague answers as equally important as the solid one.

□ **Assertion/Conclusion**

It is important to note that answers we have found can be changed according to the surrounding context and background information; that is, in fact, there is no single concrete answer in our world of uncertainty.

Fill in the blank by using easier and simpler vocabulary and expressions you can think of.

Try to find easier vocabulary and expressions for the blank than you have written previously. You can see what is academic and what is casual. This practice enhances your memory of the words and its practicality. You can also have a clear understanding for the synonyms.

Title Theorization Ethics
Course Statistics

□ Fact/Introduction

To ______________ to the _______ question, we should _____ _________ as much as possible. Then, we should ______ the _______ ________; hypothesize, conduct a research, _____ when necessary, and ______.

□ Explanation/Body

The _____ we should ____________ is that a _______ _____ doesn't always _______ a _______ answer. Therefore, we should ____ even _____ answers as equally important as the _____ one.

□ Assertion/Conclusion

It is ________ to ____ that answers we _________ can be _______ ________ __ the surrounding ______ and background information; that is, in fact, there is no _____ ______ answer in our ________________.

Guide Article

Compare the vocabulary and phrases here with those you have used previously. Many students studying English say that they do not have much vocabulary. No! That is not true at all. The reason they feel this way is that they do not have enough experiences of substituting vocabulary and phrases for others. Vocabulary and phrases takes huge parts for your writing.

Title Theorization Ethics
Course Statistics

□ Fact/Introduction

To [be closer] to the [unclear] question, we should [collect] [data] as much as possible. Then, we should [keep] the [usual] [process]; hypothesize, conduct a research, [edit] when necessary, and [make a theory].

□ Explanation/Body

The [thing] we should [remember] is that a [good] [idea] doesn't always [promise] a [specific] answer. Therefore, we should [care] even [unclear] answers as equally important as the [correct] one.

□ Assertion/Conclusion

It is [necessary] to [mention] that answers we [got] can be [revised] [by] the surrounding [condition] and background information; that is, in fact, there is no [one unchangeable] answer in our [uncertain world].

Absorb Vocabulary and Expressions

What can be used as a substitute of the word and phrase below?
Feel free to refer to the previous article.

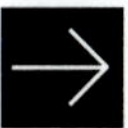

Example unclear → **uncertain**

collect →

data →

usual process →

edit →

make a theory →

the thing →

remember →

good idea →

promise →

specific answer →

care →

unclear answers →

correct →

It is necessary →

mention →

be revised by →

surrounding condition →

one unchangeable answer →

uncertain world →

Create Your Own Sentence

-Make a sentence that contains the given word and phrase.
-Use the given words for any parts of speech such as a subject, verb, object, preposition object etc.
-You can change the form of the words.

1 uncertain question

▸

2 procedure

▸

3 conduct

▸

4 keep in mind

▸

5 educated guess

▸

6. concrete

▸

7 vague

▸

8 equally important

▸

9 solid

▸

10 background information

▸

Rephrase the colored words and phrases

Change the colored words and expressions to more difficult and academic ones!
Knowing only one word for the writing will limit your skill, so you should have the alternatives.
This practice will lead you to the state-of-art academic and formal writing.

\> **Excellent**

A survey is a research way in which people who are tested respond

\>> **Impressive & Exceptional**

▶

\> **Excellent**

to a chain of explanation or questions in an enqute or an interview.

\>> **Impressive & Exceptional**

▶

You can find more reading materials in this website and expand your knowledge for the rapidly changing world.

http://www.prisonexp.org

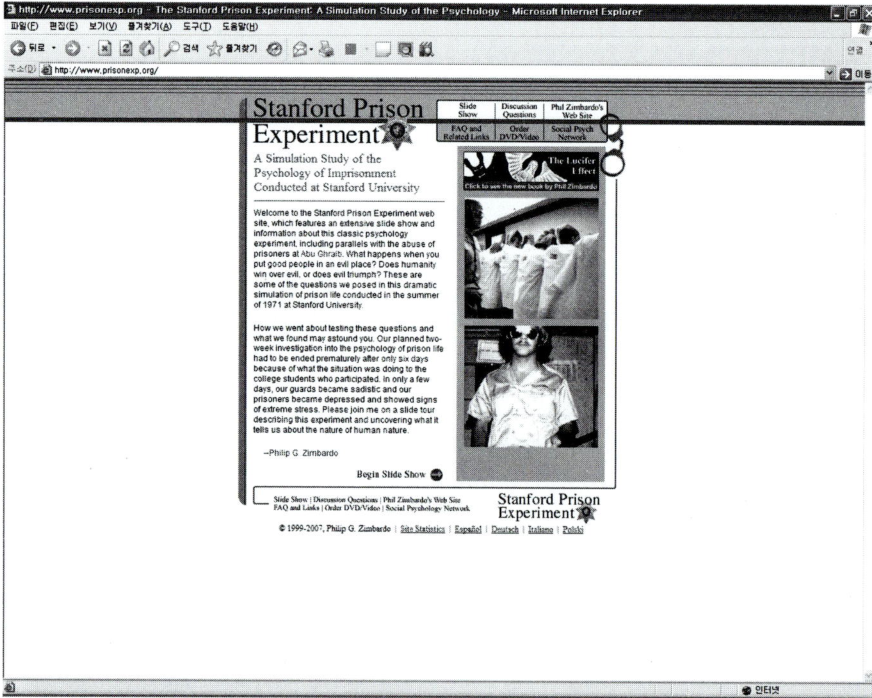

Level

Junior in University
TOEFL 6.0
3 years of studying in English speaking countries

Approximate word counts

97 words

Required Skill

Moderate level of words, but used in the academic level
"characteristics," "according to," "taste," "deepened," "conveniences," "device," "facilities," "formation."

Target 03

Higher educational institutions and elite organizations require this level of writing!

The purpose of this practice is to have you experience the high level of writing and ready for the studying in a higher educational institution. You may find it extremely difficult in choosing right words and appropriate grammar while translating the given contents.
Consult "Vocabulary You Should Know!"

Title 현대 생활에서 변화와 그 원인
Course 사회과학

□ **Fact/Introduction**

현대 생활이 가지고 있는 특징들 가운데 하나는 문화의 공유(共有)입니다.

□ **Explanation/Body**

서로 다른 문화에서 살고있는 사람들이 그들의 취향에 따라 같은 문화를 즐기는 시대가 되었습니다. 시간이 지남에 따라 다른 문화에 대한 이해가 깊어졌으며 타(他) 문화권을 받아들이려는 움직임도 활발해 졌습니다. 이러한 변화의 이면(裏面)에는 빠른 교통 수단으로 인한 여행의 간편함, 국경을 넘어선 교역, 그리고 통신설비의 발달이 있습니다.

□ **Assertion/Conclusion**

통신시설의 발달은 새로운 인간관계의 형성(形成)에 그 어느 때보다 더 많은 힘을 더할 것입니다.

Vocabulary You Should Know!

The listed vocabulary follows the sequence of the content, not randomly mixed. This will help you find the appropriate vocabulary for your writing. Vocabulary here is not only helpful for the given writing but also leading you to the place where you are to be intelligent and educated. Remember that they are the suggestions. You can have your own choices of vocabulary for the writing which might be more acceptable than the suggested one.

▷ characteristics

▷ modern

▷ sharing

▷ taste

▷ with times

▷ deepened

▷ movement

▷ embracing

▷ inside facts

▷ conveniences

▷ fast-moving transportation

▷ trades

▷ beyond

▷ border

▷ communication device

▷ facilities

▷ fuel

▷ formation

Read the following article and compare with your writing. As you read through, try to memorize the colored words and expressions.

This is one of the translations for the given material. It is worth noting that many expressions used here are the professional level. Since you are assumed to write it in your own level, you should not blame yourself when you see differences between your writing and this article.

Title Changes in Modern life and its cause
Course Social Science

□ **Fact/Introduction**

One of the characteristics that the modern life has is sharing of cultures.

□ **Explanation/Body**

It has become a time that people living in a culture different from another enjoy the same culture according to their taste. With times, understanding of other cultures has been deepened and the movement of embracing other cultural elements/area has become active. In inside facts of this change, there are conveniences of traveling by the fast-moving transportation, trades beyond the border, and developments of the communication device.

□ **Assertion/Conclusion**

The development of communication facilities will add fuel more than ever to the formation of the new human relationship.

Fill in the blank by using easier and simpler vocabulary and expressions you can think of.

Try to find easier vocabulary and expressions for the blank than you have written previously. You can see what is academic and what is casual. This practice enhances your memory of the words and its practicality. You can also have a clear understanding for the synonyms.

Title Changes in Modern life and its cause
Course Social Science

□ Fact/Introduction

One of the ____________ that the ______ life has is ______ of cultures.

□ Explanation/Body

It has become a time that people living in a culture different from another _____ the same culture according to their ____. _________, ____________ of other cultures has been ________ and the _________ of __________ other cultural ____________ has become _____. In inside facts of this change, there are ____________ of _________ by the fast-moving _____________, trades ______ the border, and ____________ of the communication _____.

□ Assertion/Conclusion

The development of communication ________ will add ____ more than ever to the _________ of the new human __________.

Guide Article

Compare the vocabulary and phrases here with those you have used previously. Many students studying English say that they do not have much vocabulary. No! That is not true at all. The reason they feel this way is that they do not have enough experiences of substituting vocabulary and phrases for others. Vocabulary and phrases takes huge parts for your writing.

Title Changes in Modern life and its cause
Course Social Science

□ **Fact/Introduction**

One of the [distinctions] that the [present] life has is [joining] of cultures.

□ **Explanation/Body**

It has become a time that people living in a culture different from another [like] the same culture according to their [preference]. [As time goes by], [knowing] of other cultures has been [grown] and the [trend] of [accepting] other cultural [objects] has become [quick]. In inside facts of this change, there are [advantages] of [having a trip] by the fast-moving [vehicle], trades [over] the border, and [advancements] of the communication [inventions].

□ **Assertion/Conclusion**

The development of communication [modes] will add [power] more than ever to the [shape] of the new human [relation/connection].

Absorb Vocabulary and Expressions

What can be used as a substitute of the word and phrase below?
Feel free to refer to the previous article.

Example distinctions → **characteristics**

present life →

preference →

As time goes by →

trend →

accepting →

objects →

quick →

advantages →

vehicle →

trades over →

advancements →

communication modes →

power →

shape →

Create Your Own Sentence

-Make a sentence that contains the given word and phrase.
-Use the given words for any parts of speech such as a subject, verb, object, preposition object etc.
-You can change the form of the words.

1 characteristics

▶

2 different from

▶

3 deepen

▶

4 embrace

▶

5 conveniences

▶

6. fast-moving transportation

▶

7 device

▶

8 facilities

▶

9 fuel

▶

10 formation

▶

Rephrase the colored words and phrases

Change the colored words and expressions to more difficult and academic ones!
Knowing only one word for the writing will limit your skill, so you should have the alternatives.
This practice will lead you to the state-of-art academic and formal writing.

> Excellent

Think the apparently personal concern of deciding to change one's name,

>> Impressive & Exceptional

▸

> Excellent

a practice very common among stars. But are the names

>> Impressive & Exceptional

▸

> Excellent

famous people use a thing of person's choice or are social pushes at work?

>> Impressive & Exceptional

▸

You can find more reading materials in this website and expand your knowledge for the rapidly changing world.

http://www.lonelyplanet.com/

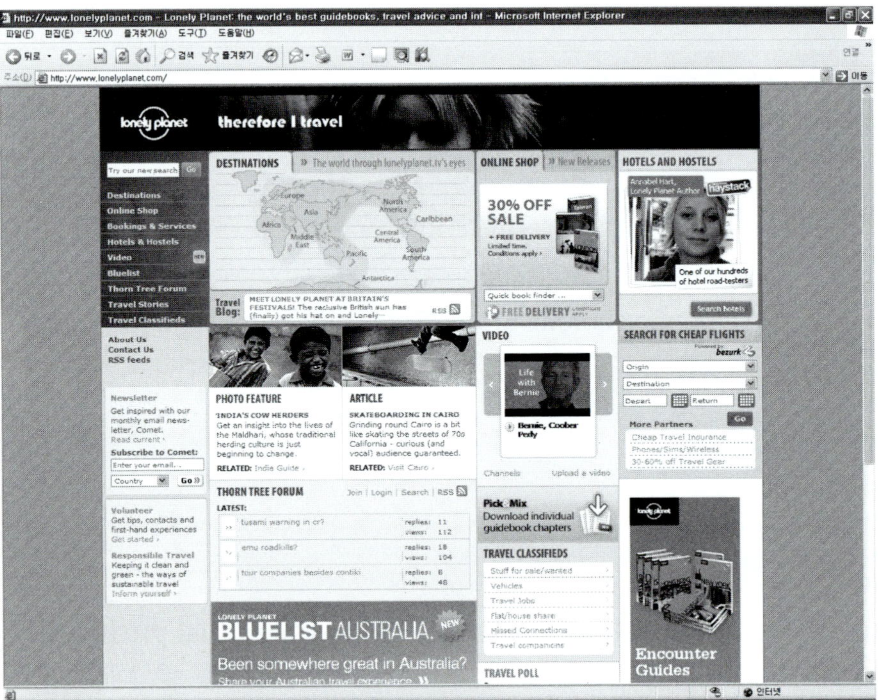

Level

Sophomore in University
TOEFL 6.0
10 month~1 year of studying in English speaking countries

Approximate word counts

102 words

Required Skill

Moderate level in word choices.
Demonstrating the fundamental level of grammar use.

Target 04

Higher educational institutions and elite organizations require this level of writing!

The purpose of this practice is to have you experience the high level of writing and ready for the studying in a higher educational institution. You may find it extremely difficult in choosing right words and appropriate grammar while translating the given contents.
Consult "Vocabulary You Should Know!"

Title 국제관계의 중요성
Course 국제 정치

□ **Fact/Introduction**

국제관계가 개인적인 단계에서는 중요하지 않을지도 모릅니다, 그러나 멀리 떨어진 나라에서 일어나는 일은 우리나라에서 삶의 질(質)과 직접적으로 연결되어 있습니다.

□ **Explanation/Body**

국제간의 연결과 그에 따른 사람들의 의존성은 우리의 부모세대와는 전혀 다른 세상을 만들어냈습니다. 이러한 상호의존성에 대한 깨달음은 결코 간과되거나 과소평가되어서는 안됩니다, 왜냐하면 그것이 앞으로 우리가 사는 방식에 지대한 영향을 미칠 것이고 또 미칠 수밖에 없기 때문입니다.

□ **Assertion/Conclusion**

좋은 국제관계를 유지하고 키워나가는 것은 모든 나라들에서 항상 최우선 과제가 되어왔습니다. 이러한 우선 과제들은 오늘날 우리가 살고 있는 현대 세상에서 더욱더 강조되고 있습니다.

Vocabulary You Should Know!

The listed vocabulary follows the sequence of the content, not randomly mixed. This will help you find the appropriate vocabulary for your writing. Vocabulary here is not only helpful for the given writing but also leading you to the place where you are to be intelligent and educated. Remember that they are the suggestions. You can have your own choices of vocabulary for the writing which might be more acceptable than the suggested one.

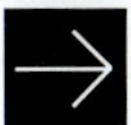

- ▷ international relations
- ▷ seem
- ▷ unimportant
- ▷ individual
- ▷ far-flung lands
- ▷ directly
- ▷ quality
- ▷ connection
- ▷ subsequent
- ▷ reliance
- ▷ in no way
- ▷ resembles
- ▷ generation
- ▷ awareness
- ▷ interdependence
- ▷ overlooked
- ▷ underestimated
- ▷ dramatically
- ▷ affect
- ▷ fostering
- ▷ maintaining
- ▷ near the top
- ▷ agenda
- ▷ priorities
- ▷ highlighted

Read the following article and compare with your writing. As you read through, try to memorize the colored words and expressions.

This is one of the translations for the given material. It is worth noting that many expressions used here are the professional level. Since you are assumed to write it in your own level, you should not blame yourself when you see differences between your writing and this article.

Title The importance of International relations
Course International Politics

□ Fact/Introduction

The international relations may seem unimportant at the individual level, but what happens in far-flung lands is connected directly to the quality of life in our own countries.

□ Explanation/Body

International connection and people's subsequent reliance on it has created a world that in no way resembles that of our parents' generation. This awareness of interdependence cannot be overlooked or underestimated because it will, and should, dramatically affect the way we live.

□ Assertion/Conclusion

Fostering and maintaining of positive international relations have always been near the top of the agenda for all nations. These priorities have become even more highlighted in the modern world that we live in today.

Fill in the blank by using easier and simpler vocabulary and expressions you can think of.

Try to find easier vocabulary and expressions for the blank than you have written previously. You can see what is academic and what is casual. This practice enhances your memory of the words and its practicality. You can also have a clear understanding for the synonyms.

Title The importance of International relations
Course International Politics

□ Fact/Introduction

The international _______ may seem unimportant at the ________ ____, but what happens in ____________ is connected directly to the ______ of life in our own countries.

□ Explanation/Body

International connection and people's _________ _______ on it has ______ a world that __ ______ ________ that of our parents' _________. This _________ of ______________ cannot be __________ or _____________ because it will, and should, __________ affect the way we live.

□ Assertion/Conclusion

________ and ___________ of _______ __________ _______ have always been ___ ___________ ______ for all ______. These ________ have become even more _________ in the modern world that we live in today.

Guide Article

Compare the vocabulary and phrases here with those you have used previously. Many students studying English say that they do not have much vocabulary. No! That is not true at all. The reason they feel this way is that they do not have enough experiences of substituting vocabulary and phrases for others. Vocabulary and phrases takes huge parts for your writing.

Title The importance of International relations
Course International Politics

□ **Fact/Introduction**

The international condition may seem unimportant at the personal situation, but what happens in the countries far away from us is connected directly to the condition of life in our own countries.

□ **Explanation/Body**

International connection and people's following dependence on it has made a world that is never similar to that of our parents' time. This realization of interrelations cannot be missed or treated easily because it will, and should, greatly affect the way we live.

□ **Assertion/Conclusion**

Developing and keeping of good world relationships have always been the most important issue for all countries. These top concerns have become even more emphasized in the modern world that we live in today.

Absorb Vocabulary and Expressions

What can be used as a substitute of the word and phrase below?
Feel free to refer to the previous article.

Example condition → **quality**

personal situation →

the countries far away from us →

people's following →

dependence →

made →

never →

similar to →

parents' time →

realization →

interrelations →

missed →

treated easily →

greatly affect →

Developing and keeping →

good world relationships →

issue →

top concerns →

emphasized →

Create Your Own Sentence

-Make a sentence that contains the given word and phrase.
-Use the given words for any parts of speech such as a subject, verb, object, preposition object etc.
-You can change the form of the words.

1 international relation

▸

2 individual level

▸

3 far-flung land

▸

4 resembles

▸

5 interdependence

▸

6. underestimate

▸

7 dramatically

▸

8 foster

▸

9 agenda

▸

10 highlight

▸

Rephrase the colored words and phrases

Change the colored words and expressions to more difficult and academic ones!
Knowing only one word for the writing will limit your skill, so you should have the alternatives.
This practice will lead you to the state-of-art academic and formal writing.

> Excellent

Our political structure is based on the standard of free elections just as

>> Impressive & Exceptional

▶

> Excellent

we believe that our economy react to the necessities and choices of customers.

>> Impressive & Exceptional

▶

You can find more reading materials in this website and expand your knowledge for the rapidly changing world.

http://www.un.org/

Level

Sophomore in University
TOEFL 6.0
1 year of studying in English speaking countries

Approximate word counts

104 words

Required Skill

Demonstrating the fundamental level of grammar use. Academic expressions and phrases with "be preserved," "reluctant to," "formal education," "display," "indifference," "Two thirds of," "curriculums/curricula," "deals with," "expansion of," "rise of," "weakened," "the value of," "flood tide," "mammonism," "a success-at-all-cost," "accelerate," "erosion of."

Target 05

Higher educational institutions and elite organizations require this level of writing!

The purpose of this practice is to have you experience the high level of writing and ready for the studying in a higher educational institution. You may find it extremely difficult in choosing right words and appropriate grammar while translating the given contents.
Consult "Vocabulary You Should Know!"

Title 전통, 우리는 더 이상 가르치지 않는다
Course 대중 교육

□ Fact/Introduction

사람들은 전통이 보존되고 전수되어야 한다는 것에 동의합니다. 그러나, 정규 교육을 통해서 전통을 가르치는 것에 대해서 그들은 마음이 내키지 않는 듯합니다.

□ Explanation/Body

사람들은 그들의 문화와 관습을 적극적으로 가르치는 것에 무관심한 태도를 보입니다. 학교 교과 과정의 3분의 2가 과학, 수학, 정치, 물리, 그리고 화학 과목을 포함하고 있습니다. 단지 3분의 1만이 전통과 관습에 관련된 과목을 다루고 있습니다. 도시의 확장과 산업경제의 등장이 전통의 가치를 약화시키고 있음에도 불구하고 학교 교육은 이러한 변화에 효과적으로 대처하고 있지 않습니다.

□ Assertion/Conclusion

게다가, 황금만능주의의 팽배는 무슨 수를 써서라도 성공해야 한다는 생활양식으로 우리를 유도하고 있습니다. 이러한 모든 것이 전통의 붕괴를 가속화 하고 있습니다.

Vocabulary You Should Know!

The listed vocabulary follows the sequence of the content, not randomly mixed. This will help you find the appropriate vocabulary for your writing. Vocabulary here is not only helpful for the given writing but also leading you to the place where you are to be intelligent and educated. Remember that they are the suggestions. You can have your own choices of vocabulary for the writing which might be more acceptable than the suggested one.

- ▷ reluctant
- ▷ formal education
- ▷ display
- ▷ indifference
- ▷ curriculums/curricula
- ▷ subjects
- ▷ deals with
- ▷ related with
- ▷ expansion
- ▷ rise
- ▷ weakened
- ▷ school education
- ▷ effectively
- ▷ cope with
- ▷ flood tide
- ▷ mammonism
- ▷ success-at-all-cost
- ▷ accelerate
- ▷ erosion

Read the following article and compare with your writing. As you read through, try to memorize the colored words and expressions.

This is one of the translations for the given material. It is worth noting that many expressions used here are the professional level. Since you are assumed to write it in your own level, you should not blame yourself when you see differences between your writing and this article.

Title Tradition, We do not teach anymore
Course Public Education

□ Fact/Introduction

People agree that traditions should be preserved and taught. However, they seem reluctant to teach traditions through the formal education.

□ Explanation/Body

People display indifference toward the active teaching of their culture and customs. Two thirds of school curriculums/curricula include the subjects of science, mathematics, politics, physics, and chemistry. Only one third deals with the subjects related with traditions and costumes. Although the expansion of cities and the rise of an industrial economy have weakened the value of the traditions, school education does not effectively cope with these changes.

□ Assertion/Conclusion

Moreover, the flood tide of mammonism guides us to a success-at-all-cost lifestyle. All these accelerate the erosion of the traditions.

Fill in the blank by using easier and simpler vocabulary and expressions you can think of.

Try to find easier vocabulary and expressions for the blank than you have written previously. You can see what is academic and what is casual. This practice enhances your memory of the words and its practicality. You can also have a clear understanding for the synonyms.

Title Tradition, We do not teach anymore
Course Public Education

□ **Fact/Introduction**

People agree that traditions should be ________ and taught. ________, they seem ________ to teach traditions through the ______ education.

□ **Explanation/Body**

People ______ __________ ______ the active teaching of their culture and ______. Two thirds of school ________________ ______ the ______ of science, mathematics, politics, physics, and chemistry. Only one third ____ ____ the subjects ______ with traditions and costumes. Although the ________ of cities and the ____ of an industrial economy have ________ the ____ of the traditions, school education does not ________ ________ these changes.

□ **Assertion/Conclusion**

________, the ________ of ___________ ______ us to a success-at-all-cost ______. All these ________ the ______ of the traditions.

Guide Article

Compare the vocabulary and phrases here with those you have used previously. Many students studying English say that they do not have much vocabulary. No! That is not true at all. The reason they feel this way is that they do not have enough experiences of substituting vocabulary and phrases for others. Vocabulary and phrases takes huge parts for your writing.

Title Tradition, We do not teach anymore
Course Public Education

□ Fact/Introduction

People agree that traditions should be [protected] and taught. [But], they seem [unwilling] to teach traditions through the [regular] education.

□ Explanation/Body

People [show] [carelessness] [to] the active teaching of their culture and [traditions]. Two thirds of school [courses] [have] the [class] of science, mathematics, politics, physics, and chemistry. Only one third [teaches] the subjects [connected] with traditions and costumes. Although the [growth] of cities and the [development] of an industrial economy have [damaged] the [importance] of the traditions, school education does not [efficiently] [respond to] these changes.

□ Assertion/Conclusion

[Furthermore], the [expansion] of [the almighty dollar principle] [leads] us to a success-at-all-cost [style of living]. All these [speed up] the [disappearance] of the traditions.

Absorb Vocabulary and Expressions

What can be used as a substitute of the word and phrase below?
Feel free to refer to the previous article.

Example protected → **preserved**

unwilling →

regular education →

show →

carelessness to →

traditions →

courses have →

teaches →

connected with →

growth →

development →

damaged →

importance →

efficiently →

respond to →

expansion →

the almighty dollar principle →

leads →

style of living →

speed up →

disappearance →

Create Your Own Sentence

-Make a sentence that contains the given word and phrase.
-Use the given words for any parts of speech such as a subject, verb, object, preposition object etc.
-You can change the form of the words.

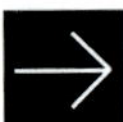

1 indifference

▶

2 expansion

▶

3 weaken

▶

4 school education

▶

5 cope with

▶

6. flood tide

▶

7 mammonism

▶

8 success-at-all-cost

▶

9 accelerate

▶

10 erosion

▶

Rephrase the colored words and phrases

Change the colored words and expressions to more difficult and academic ones!
Knowing only one word for the writing will limit your skill, so you should have the alternatives.
This practice will lead you to the state-of-art academic and formal writing.

→

> Excellent

The students of the 1990s look much more interested in being rich financially,

>> Impressive & Exceptional

▶

> Excellent

while their opposite students in the late 1960s focused on learning a philosophy of life.

>> Impressive & Exceptional

▶

You can find more reading materials in this website and expand your knowledge for the rapidly changing world.

http://www.ed.gov/index.jhtml

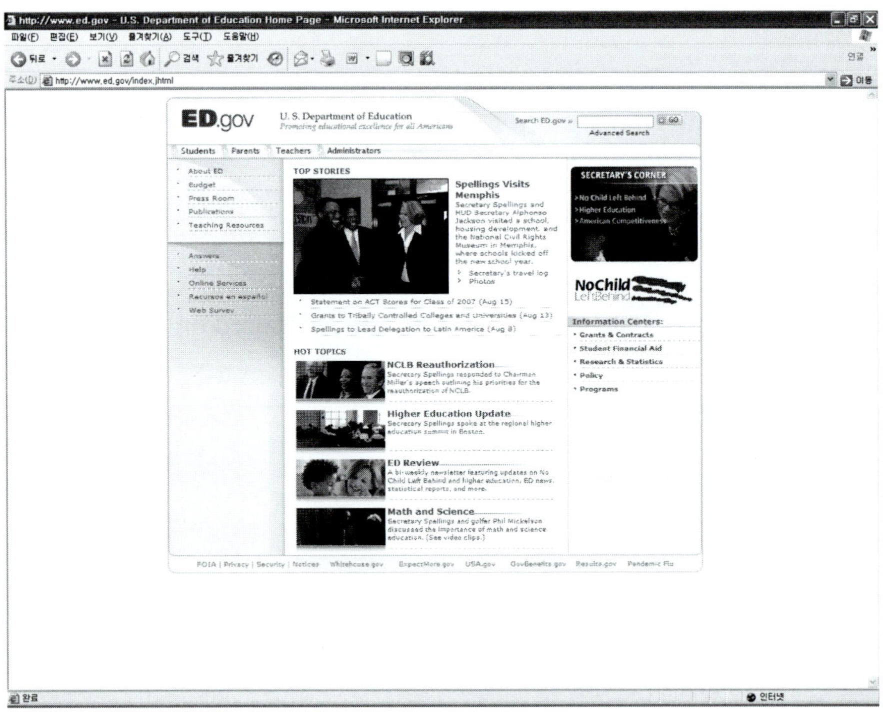

Level

Junior in University
TOEFL 6.0
2~3 years of studying in English speaking countries

Approximate word counts

107 words

Required Skill

Economical words and terminologies are required in using "Financial markets," "stock price," "floating," "rises and falls," "oil prices," "fluctuations," "specialists," "monitor," "variable," "determines," "invisible," "skillful."

Target 06

Higher educational institutions and elite organizations require this level of writing!

The purpose of this practice is to have you experience the high level of writing and ready for the studying in a higher educational institution. You may find it extremely difficult in choosing right words and appropriate grammar while translating the given contents.
Consult "Vocabulary You Should Know!"

Title 금융시장, 눈에 보이지 않는 정보
Course 국제경제

□ **Fact/Introduction**

금융시장은 매우 유동적(流動的)입니다. 국제정치의 변화 그리고 석유가격의 등락과 같은 국제정세는 주가변동에 큰 영향을 줍니다.

□ **Explanation/Body**

금융 전문가들은 또한 국제경제에 영향을 미칠지도 모르는 다른 변수들을 예의 주시합니다.
석유가격 이외에 경제에 영향력을 행사하는 것은 곡물의 가격입니다. 어떻게 곡물의 가격이 책정되는지가 수출입 가격을 결정합니다.
이러한 눈에 보이지 않는 변화들은 이러한 눈에 보이지 않는 정보에 접근할 수 있는 사람들에게 혜택을 줍니다.

□ **Assertion/Conclusion**

그러므로, 노련한 투자자들은 그들에게 직접 또는 간접적으로 영향을 줄 수 있는 국제 정보의 흐름을 주시해서 봅니다.

Vocabulary You Should Know!

The listed vocabulary follows the sequence of the content, not randomly mixed. This will help you find the appropriate vocabulary for your writing. Vocabulary here is not only helpful for the given writing but also leading you to the place where you are to be intelligent and educated. Remember that they are the suggestions. You can have your own choices of vocabulary for the writing which might be more acceptable than the suggested one.

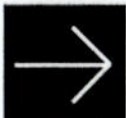

▷ Financial markets
▷ floating
▷ International situations
▷ such as ~
▷ the international politics
▷ rises and falls
▷ oil prices
▷ impact on
▷ stock price
▷ fluctuations
▷ specialists
▷ monitoring
▷ variables
▷ influence
▷ international economy
▷ besides
▷ grain
▷ exercises ~ influence
▷ be measured
▷ determines
▷ import and export
▷ invisible
▷ benefit
▷ access
▷ Therefore
▷ skillful
▷ investors
▷ note
▷ information flow
▷ direct
▷ indirect
▷ effect

Read the following article and compare with your writing. As you read through, try to memorize the colored words and expressions.

This is one of the translations for the given material. It is worth noting that many expressions used here are the professional level. Since you are assumed to write it in your own level, you should not blame yourself when you see differences between your writing and this article.

Title Financial Market, Invisible Information
Course International Economy

□ **Fact/Introduction**

Financial markets are very floating. International situations such as changes in the international politics, and rises and falls in the oil prices have a great impact on stock price fluctuations.

□ **Explanation/Body**

Financial specialists are also monitoring the other variables that might influence the international economy.

Besides the oil prices, it is the price of the grain that exercises its influence over the economy. How the price of the grain is measured determines the import and export price.

These invisible changes benefit the people who have the access to this invisible information.

□ **Assertion/Conclusion**

Therefore, skillful investors note the international information flow that could have a direct or an indirect effect on them.

Fill in the blank by using easier and simpler vocabulary and expressions you can think of.

Try to find easier vocabulary and expressions for the blank than you have written previously. You can see what is academic and what is casual. This practice enhances your memory of the words and its practicality. You can also have a clear understanding for the synonyms.

Title Financial Market, Invisible Information
Course International Economy

□ Fact/Introduction

Financial markets are very ______. International ______ such as changes in the ______ politics, and ______ in the oil prices have a ______ impact on stock price ______.

□ Explanation/Body

Financial ______ are also ______ the other ______ that might ______ the international economy.
______ the oil prices, it is the price of the ______ that ______ its influence over the economy. ______ the price of the ______ is ______ ______ the import and export price.
These ______ changes ______ the people who have the ______ to this ______ information.

□ Assertion/Conclusion

Therefore, ______ ______ ______ the international information ______ that could have a ______ effect on them.

Guide Article

Compare the vocabulary and phrases here with those you have used previously. Many students studying English say that they do not have much vocabulary. No! That is not true at all. The reason they feel this way is that they do not have enough experiences of substituting vocabulary and phrases for others. Vocabulary and phrases takes huge parts for your writing.

Title Financial Market, Invisible Information
Course International Economy

□ Fact/Introduction

Financial markets are very unstable. International conditions such as changes in the world politics and unpredictable changes in the oil prices have a big impact on stock price changes.

□ Explanation/Body

Financial experts are also checking the other elements that might control the international economy.

In addition to the oil prices, it is the price of the rice that affects its influence over the economy. The way the price of the rice is estimated decides the import and export price.

These hidden changes give a benefit to the people who have the door to this hidden information.

□ Assertion/Conclusion

Therefore, smart businessmen notice the international information move that could have a significant effect on them.

Absorb Vocabulary and Expressions

What can be used as a substitute of the word and phrase below?
Feel free to refer to the previous article.

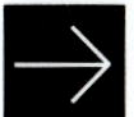

Example unstable → **floating**

conditions →

world politics →

unpredictable changes →

big →

changes →

financial experts →

checking →

elements →

control →

In addition to →

rice →

affects →

estimated →

decides →

hidden →

give a benefit to →

door →

hidden information →

smart →

businessmen →

notice →

information move →

significant →

Create Your Own Sentence

-Make a sentence that contains the given word and phrase.
-Use the given words for any parts of speech such as a subject, verb, object, preposition object etc.
-You can change the form of the words.

1 markets

▶

2 international politics

▶

3 rises and falls

▶

4 stock price

▶

5 international economy

▶

6. oil prices

▶

7 import and export

▶

8 information

▶

9 investors

▶

10 direct effect

▶

Rephrase the colored words and phrases

Change the colored words and expressions to more difficult and academic ones!
Knowing only one word for the writing will limit your skill, so you should have the alternatives.
This practice will lead you to the state-of-art academic and formal writing.

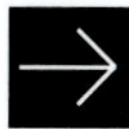

> Excellent

Besides sharing style of living, people now attend in a world economy.

>> Impressive & Exceptional

▶

> Excellent

Many independent economic systems, surrounded by national borders, have been changed by large companies

>> Impressive & Exceptional

▶

> Excellent

that produce and sell goods through the world, and money market, connected by satellite communication, work around the clock.

>> Impressive & Exceptional

▶

You can find more reading materials in this website and expand your knowledge for the rapidly changing world.

http://www.nasdaq.com/

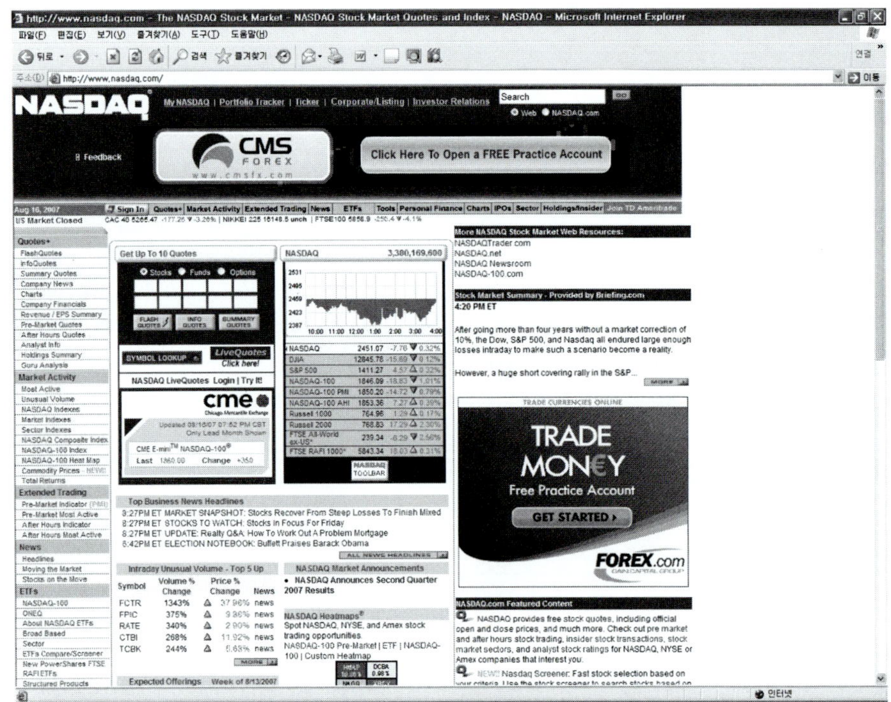

Level

Junior in University
TOEFL 6.0
2~3 years of studying in English speaking countries

Approximate word counts

110 words

Required Skill

High level in word choices and standard expressions such as "One third," "technologically," "region," "poverty," "hold," "the age of," "child labor," "burdens," "manual works," "fall on," "child abuse," "opposing."

Target 07

Higher educational institutions and elite organizations require this level of writing!

The purpose of this practice is to have you experience the high level of writing and ready for the studying in a higher educational institution. You may find it extremely difficult in choosing right words and appropriate grammar while translating the given contents.
Consult "Vocabulary You Should Know!"

Title 미성년 노동 보고서
Course 평화교육

□ Fact/Introduction

세계 국가들의 3분의 1이 기술적으로 단순한 수준의 사회에 해당됩니다. 이러한 지역에 있는 아이들은 많은 양의 가사(家事)로부터 자유롭지 못합니다.

□ Explanation/Body

빈곤 속에 있는 아이들은 그들의 가족에 대한 책임을 지게 됩니다. 어떤 경우에는, 가족을 부양하기 위해서 12살의 아이들이 군대에 갈 것을 요구당하기도 합니다. 이러한 가난한 사회들은 국가 기반산업의 건설을 위해서 미성년 노동에 의지하는 경우가 비일비재(非一非再)합니다.
잘 사는 나라와 못 사는 나라 사이의 차이가 커짐에 따라 중노동의 부담감은 아이들에게 떨어집니다.

□ Assertion/Conclusion

최근에 UNICEF가 이러한 불법 아동 학대를 중지시키고 인신매매를 근절시키기 위해서 노력하고 있습니다. 하지만, 몇몇 나라들은 UNICEF의 접근을 적극적으로 반대하고 있습니다.

Vocabulary You Should Know!

The listed vocabulary follows the sequence of the content, not randomly mixed. This will help you find the appropriate vocabulary for your writing. Vocabulary here is not only helpful for the given writing but also leading you to the place where you are to be intelligent and educated. Remember that they are the suggestions. You can have your own choices of vocabulary for the writing which might be more acceptable than the suggested one.

▷ one third
▷ belongs to
▷ technologically
▷ simple society
▷ region
▷ great deal
▷ housework
▷ poverty
▷ hold
▷ responsibility
▷ join
▷ support
▷ frequently
▷ child labor
▷ national
▷ chief industries
▷ gap
▷ widen
▷ burdens
▷ heavy
▷ manual works
▷ recently
▷ illegal
▷ child abuse
▷ eradicate
▷ human traffic
▷ active
▷ approach

Read the following article and compare with your writing. As you read through, try to memorize the colored words and expressions.

This is one of the translations for the given material. It is worth noting that many expressions used here are the professional level. Since you are assumed to write it in your own level, you should not blame yourself when you see differences between your writing and this article.

Title Report of Child Labor
Course Peace Education

□ Fact/Introduction

One third of the world's nations belongs to the technologically simple society. Children in this region are not free from the great deal of housework.

□ Explanation/Body

Children in poverty hold a responsibility for their family. In some cases, children in the age of 12 are told to join the army to support the family. These poor societies frequently depend on the child labor to build the national chief industries.

As the gap between rich and poor has become widen, the burdens of heavy manual works fall on the children.

□ Assertion/Conclusion

UNICEF is recently trying to stop this illegal child abuse and eradicate human traffic. However, some countries are active in opposing its approach.

Fill in the blank by using easier and simpler vocabulary and expressions you can think of.

Try to find easier vocabulary and expressions for the blank than you have written previously. You can see what is academic and what is casual. This practice enhances your memory of the words and its practicality. You can also have a clear understanding for the synonyms.

Title Report of Child Labor
Course Peace Education

□ Fact/Introduction

One third of the world's nations belongs to the ____________ ______ society. Children in this ______ are not free from the ___________ housework.

□ Explanation/Body

Children in ______ ____ a __________ for their family. In some cases, children in the age of 12 are ___ to ___ the army to ______ the family. These poor societies frequently ______ on the child labor to ____ the national chief industries.

As the ___ between rich and poor has become _____, the ______ of _____ _____ works fall on the children.

□ Assertion/Conclusion

UNICEF is recently trying to stop this illegal child abuse and _______ human traffic. However, some countries are active in _______ its _______

Guide Article

Compare the vocabulary and phrases here with those you have used previously. Many students studying English say that they do not have much vocabulary. No! That is not true at all. The reason they feel this way is that they do not have enough experiences of substituting vocabulary and phrases for others. Vocabulary and phrases takes huge parts for your writing.

Title Report of Child Labor
Course Peace Education

□ **Fact/Introduction**

One third of the world's nations belongs to the scientifically backward society. Children in this area are not free from a lot of housework.

□ **Explanation/Body**

Children in poor condition have a duty for their family. In some cases, children in the age of 12 are ordered to go to the army to help the family. These poor societies frequently rely on the child labor to make the national chief industries.

As the difference between rich and poor has become bigger, the stress of difficult physical works falls on the children.

□ **Assertion/Conclusion**

UNICEF is recently trying to stop this illegal child abuse and get rid of human traffic. However, some countries are active in fighting against its coming close

Absorb Vocabulary and Expressions

What can be used as a substitute of the word and phrase below?
Feel free to refer to the previous article.

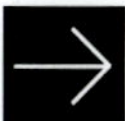

Example scientifically backward → **technologically simple**

area →

a lot of →

poor condition →

have a duty →

ordered →

help →

rely on →

make →

difference →

bigger →

stress →

difficult →

physical works →

get rid of →

coming close →

Create Your Own Sentence

-Make a sentence that contains the given word and phrase.
-Use the given words for any parts of speech such as a subject, verb, object, preposition object etc.
-You can change the form of the words.

1 world's nations

▸

2 a great deal of

▸

3 hold a responsibility

▸

4 support

▸

5 child labor

▸

6. national chief industries

▸

7 burdens

▸

8 manual works

▸

9 eradicate

▸

10 human traffic

▸

Rephrase the colored words and phrases

Change the colored words and expressions to more difficult and academic ones!
Knowing only one word for the writing will limit your skill, so you should have the alternatives.
This practice will lead you to the state-of-art academic and formal writing.

> Excellent

While a few people in the poor countries are rich,

>> Impressive & Exceptional

▶

> Excellent

the most people face the stress of living each day. These people live on

>> Impressive & Exceptional

▶

> Excellent

the limit of survival not because of any personal weakness but because of the social structure of their societies.

>> Impressive & Exceptional

▶

You can find more reading materials in this website and expand your knowledge for the rapidly changing world.

http://www.unicef.org

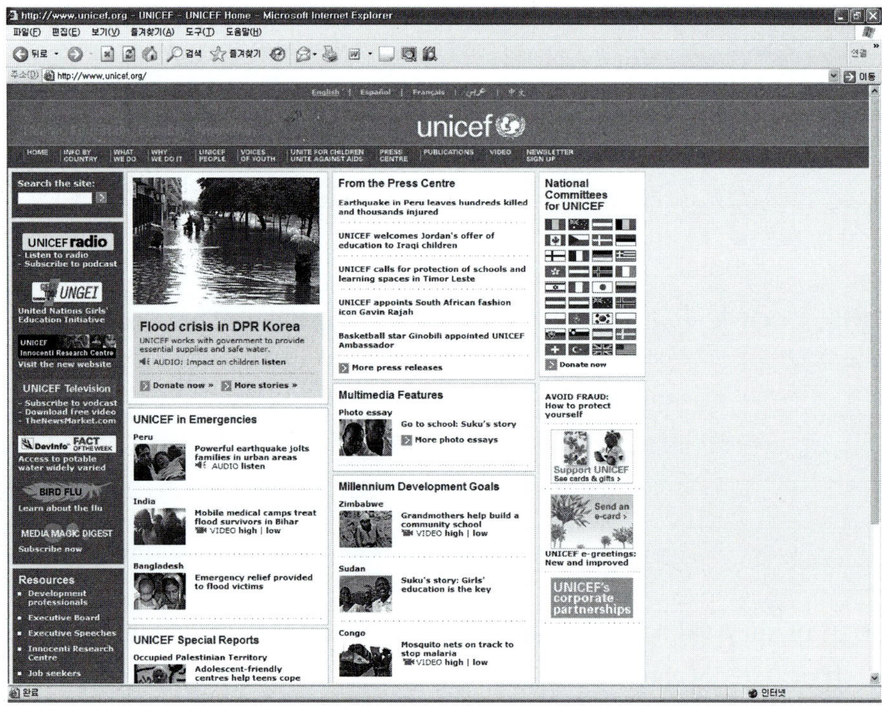

Level

Junior in University
TOEFL 6.0
2 years of studying in English speaking countries

Approximate word counts

128 words

Required Skill

Moderate level of words, but used in many academic texts
"muscle," "precision," "leading," "reacts to," "input," "racing to," "sophisticated," "provokes," "pursuit," "in check," "check and balance."

Target 08

Higher educational institutions and elite organizations require this level of writing!

The purpose of this practice is to have you experience the high level of writing and ready for the studying in a higher educational institution. You may find it extremely difficult in choosing right words and appropriate grammar while translating the given contents.
Consult "Vocabulary You Should Know!"

Title 로봇, 우리의 미래?
Course 기계공학

□ Fact/Introduction

인간은 사람들의 노동력을 정밀한 기계들로 대체하고 있습니다. 로봇들을 산업에 이용하는 것이 대표적인 예(例) 입니다.

□ Explanation/Body

요즘에는 로봇이 어디에나 있습니다. 가장 간단한 형태의 로봇인 커피 자판기에서부터 좀더 복잡한 형태의 로봇인 산업용 로봇까지 로봇들은 우리의 삶속에 깊이 들어와 있습니다. 많은 나라들은 다른 나라가 가지고 있는 것 보다 더욱 정교하고 지능적인 로봇들을 가지기 위해서 경쟁하고 있습니다. 한 나라의 로봇 공학의 발달은 자연스럽게 이웃나라의 추격을 유발(誘發)합니다. 그래서 각 나라는 서로를 견제하기 위해서 로봇학에 주력(注力)하고 있습니다.

□ Assertion/Conclusion

그러나, 경쟁적인 로봇 기술의 개발로 인해서 나라들 사이의 견제와 균형을 유지하기가 더욱 어려워지고 있습니다. 로봇들이 우리 삶의 혜택이 아니라 우리 삶의 끝을 가져올 수도 있다는 우려의 목소리도 높아지고 있습니다.

Vocabulary You Should Know!

The listed vocabulary follows the sequence of the content, not randomly mixed. This will help you find the appropriate vocabulary for your writing. Vocabulary here is not only helpful for the given writing but also leading you to the place where you are to be intelligent and educated. Remember that they are the suggestions. You can have your own choices of vocabulary for the writing which might be more acceptable than the suggested one.

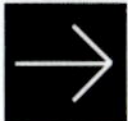

- ▷ replacing
- ▷ muscle power
- ▷ precision
- ▷ leading
- ▷ nowadays
- ▷ everywhere
- ▷ dispensers
- ▷ complex form
- ▷ deep in
- ▷ racing
- ▷ sophisticated
- ▷ robotics
- ▷ provokes
- ▷ pursuit
- ▷ concentrating
- ▷ robotology
- ▷ hold each other in check
- ▷ check and balance
- ▷ competitive
- ▷ robot technology
- ▷ concerning
- ▷ end
- ▷ benefits

Read the following article and compare with your writing. As you read through, try to memorize the colored words and expressions.

This is one of the translations for the given material. It is worth noting that many expressions used here are the professional level. Since you are assumed to write it in your own level, you should not blame yourself when you see differences between your writing and this article.

Title Robot, Our future?
Course Mechanical Engineering

□ Fact/Introduction

Human beings have been replacing the muscle power with the precision machines. Using robots in industry is the leading example.

□ Explanation/Body

Nowadays, robots are everywhere. From coffee dispensers, the simplest form of a robot, to industrial robot, the more complex form of robot, robots have entered deep in our life. Many nations are racing to have more sophisticated and intelligent robots than the others have. The development of one nation's robotics naturally provokes a neighboring nation's pursuit. Therefore, every nation is concentrating its efforts on robotology to hold each other in check.

□ Assertion/Conclusion

However, it has become more difficult to maintain check and balance between nations because of the competitive development of robot technology. A concerning voice that robots could bring our life's end, not the benefits of our life, has also arisen.

Fill in the blank by using easier and simpler vocabulary and expressions you can think of.

Try to find easier vocabulary and expressions for the blank than you have written previously. You can see what is academic and what is casual. This practice enhances your memory of the words and its practicality. You can also have a clear understanding for the synonyms.

Title Robot, Our future?
Course Mechanical Engineering

□ Fact/Introduction

__________ have been __________ the __________ power ______ the __________ machines. Using robots in __________ is the __________ example.

□ Explanation/Body

__________, robots are __________. From coffee __________, the simplest ______ of a robot, to __________ robot, the more complex form of robot, robots have entered deep in our life. Many nations __________ have more __________ and __________ robots than the others have. The development of one nation's __________ __________ __________ a __________ nation's pursuit. Therefore, every nation is __________ its efforts on __________ to hold each other in check.

□ Assertion/Conclusion

However, it __________ more __________ to __________ check and balance between nations because of the __________ development of robot technology. A __________ voice that robots could ______ our life's end, not the ______ of our life, has also arisen.

Guide Article

Compare the vocabulary and phrases here with those you have used previously. Many students studying English say that they do not have much vocabulary. No! That is not true at all. The reason they feel this way is that they do not have enough experiences of substituting vocabulary and phrases for others. Vocabulary and phrases takes huge parts for your writing.

Title Robot, Our future?
Course Mechanical Engineering

□ Fact/Introduction

Humans have been switching the men power to the accurate machines. Using robots in factories is the nice example.

□ Explanation/Body

In these days, robots are all over the place. From coffee vending machines, the simplest type of a robot, to factory robots, the more complex form of robot, robots have entered deep in our life. Many nations are competing to have more advanced and smart robots than the others have. The development of one nation's robot techniques simply stimulates a nearby nation's pursuit. Therefore, every nation is focusing its efforts on studying robots to hold each other in check.

□ Assertion/Conclusion

However, it became hard to keep check and balance between nations because of the aggressive development of robot technology. A worrying voice that robots could cause our life's end, not the advantage of our life, has also arisen.

Absorb Vocabulary and Expressions

What can be used as a substitute of the word and phrase below?
Feel free to refer to the previous article.

Example Humans → **Human beings**

switching →

men power →

accurate →

factories →

nice example →

in these days →

all over the place →

vending machines →

type →

factory robots →

are competing to →

advanced →

smart →

simply →

stimulates →

nearby →

focusing on →

studying robots →

became hard →

keep →

worrying voice →

Create Your Own Sentence

-Make a sentence that contains the given word and phrase.
-Use the given words for any parts of speech such as a subject, verb, object, preposition object etc.
-You can change the form of the words.

1 muscle power

▸

2 race

▸

3 sophisticate

▸

4 robotics

▸

5 provokes

▸

6. neighboring

▸

7 pursuit

▸

8 hold each other in check

▸

9 competitive development

▸

10 concerning voice

▸

Rephrase the colored words and phrases

Change the colored words and expressions to more difficult and academic ones!
Knowing only one word for the writing will limit your skill, so you should have the alternatives.
This practice will lead you to the state-of-art academic and formal writing.

→

> Excellent

As bones, muscles, and different inside body part of the body each

>> Impressive & Exceptional

▸

> Excellent

help to the survival of the human body, Spencer claimed, so do machine structures.

>> Impressive & Exceptional

▸

You can find more reading materials in this website and expand your knowledge for the rapidly changing world.

http://www.roboticstrends.com/

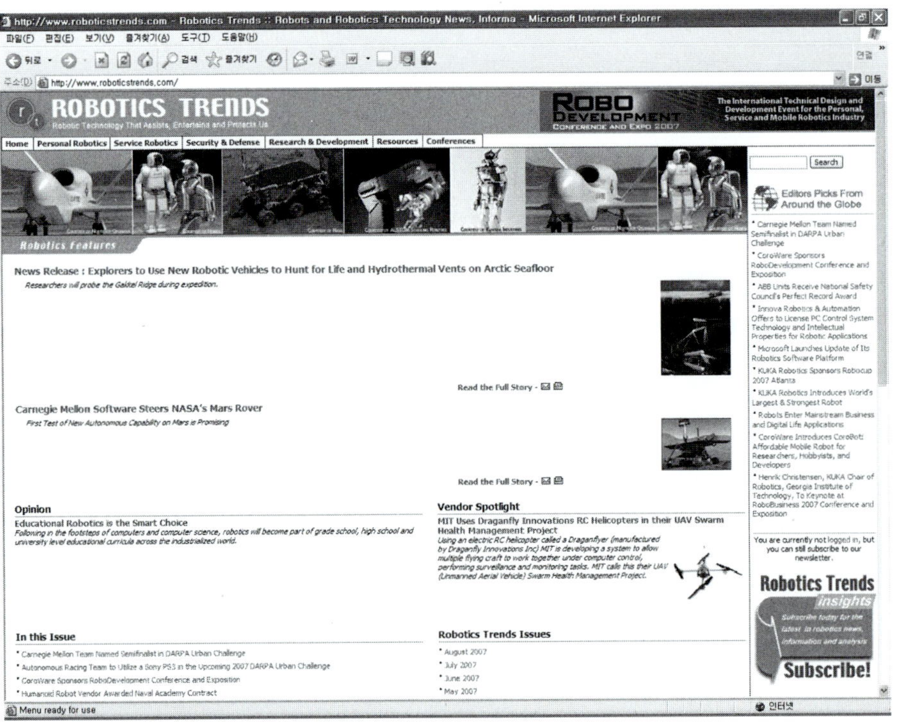

Level

Freshmen in University
TOEFL 6.0
1 ~ 1 and a half years of studying in English speaking countries

Approximate word counts

129 words

Required Skill

Use words such as, "adolescent," "immature," "excusable," "norm," "conclude," "visual scene," "unreasonable," "excessive," "merits," "slow down," and "circulation," to develop the context.

Target 09

Higher educational institutions and elite organizations require this level of writing!

The purpose of this practice is to have you experience the high level of writing and ready for the studying in a higher educational institution. You may find it extremely difficult in choosing right words and appropriate grammar while translating the given contents.
Consult "Vocabulary You Should Know!"

Title 인터넷이 성인에게 주는 영향
Course 행동 심리학

□ Fact/Introduction

성인들이 저지르는 몇몇 미숙한 행동들은 가볍게 봐줄 수 있고 심지어 귀엽기 조차 합니다. 그러나, 어떤 행동들은 공격적이고 사회규범에 어긋납니다.

□ Explanation/Body

과학자들은 성인들의 정신 발달을 방해하는 주된 요인이 인터넷 게임이라고 결론을 내렸습니다. 게임의 형태와 눈에 보이는 장면들의 영향 아래에서 성인들의 감정과 창조성은 크게 영향을 받습니다. 이런 결과는 나중에 반드시 나타납니다. 예를 들어서 회의를 지속적으로 방해하고 다른 사람들을 향하여 이유없이 공격적인 태도를 보이는 성인들은 인터넷 게임의 영향을 받고 있다고 할 수 있습니다. 더욱더 많은 성인들은 그들이 여전히 청소년 단계에 머물고 있음을 보이고 있습니다.

□ Assertion/Conclusion

결과적으로, 과도한 인터넷 게임은 정신 발달에 이로운 점이 없습니다. 더 많은 과학적인 발견들은 화면으로부터의 감마광선(gamma rays)이 뇌의 혈액 순환을 느리게 한다는 것도 보여줍니다.

Vocabulary You Should Know!

The listed vocabulary follows the sequence of the content, not randomly mixed. This will help you find the appropriate vocabulary for your writing. Vocabulary here is not only helpful for the given writing but also leading you to the place where you are to be intelligent and educated. Remember that they are the suggestions. You can have your own choices of vocabulary for the writing which might be more acceptable than the suggested one.

- ▷ immature
- ▷ behaviors
- ▷ excusable
- ▷ aggressive
- ▷ against
- ▷ norm
- ▷ conclude
- ▷ main
- ▷ influence
- ▷ visual
- ▷ emotions
- ▷ creativities
- ▷ greatly
- ▷ affected
- ▷ outcome
- ▷ certainly
- ▷ arises
- ▷ interrupting
- ▷ unreasonable
- ▷ toward
- ▷ being influenced
- ▷ adolescent
- ▷ stage
- ▷ excessive
- ▷ merits
- ▷ scientific findings
- ▷ rays
- ▷ slow down
- ▷ circulation

**Read the following article and compare with your writing.
As you read through, try to memorize the colored words and expressions.**

This is one of the translations for the given material. It is worth noting that many expressions used here are the professional level. Since you are assumed to write it in your own level, you should not blame yourself when you see differences between your writing and this article.

Title Adults under the Influence of Internet
Course Behavior Psychology

□ Fact/Introduction

Some immature behaviors done by adults are excusable and even cute. However, some are aggressive and against the norm.

□ Explanation/Body

Scientists conclude that Internet game is the main reason that bothers the mental growing of the adults. Under the influence of the game type and the visual scene, adults'emotions and creativities are greatly affected. This outcome certainly arises later. For example, adults showing continuous interrupting the meeting and unreasonable aggressive attitudes toward other people should have been being influenced by the Internet game. More and more adults are showing that they are still in the adolescent stage.

□ Assertion/Conclusion

In result, excessive playing the Internet game has no merits on the mental development. More scientific findings also show that the gamma rays from the screen slow down the blood circulation of the brain.

Fill in the blank by using easier and simpler vocabulary and expressions you can think of.

Try to find easier vocabulary and expressions for the blank than you have written previously. You can see what is academic and what is casual. This practice enhances your memory of the words and its practicality. You can also have a clear understanding for the synonyms.

Title Adults under the Influence of Internet
Course Behavior Psychology

□ Fact/Introduction

Some ________ ________ done by adults are ________ and even cute. ________, some are ________ and break the _____.

□ Explanation/Body

Scientists ________ that Internet game is the _____ reason that bothers the mental growing of the _____. Under the ________ of the game type and the visual scene, adults' ________ and creativities are ______ affected. This ________ ________ _____ later. For example, adults showing continuous __________ the meeting and ___________ _________ _______ ______ other people ______________ ______________ by the Internet game. More and more adults are showing that they are still in the ________ _____.

□ Assertion/Conclusion

In result, ________ playing the Internet game has no ______ on the mental __________. More scientific _______ also show that the gamma rays from the screen slow down the blood _________ of the brain.

Guide Article

Compare the vocabulary and phrases here with those you have used previously. Many students studying English say that they do not have much vocabulary. No! That is not true at all. The reason they feel this way is that they do not have enough experiences of substituting vocabulary and phrases for others. Vocabulary and phrases takes huge parts for your writing.

Title Adults under the Influence of Internet
Course Behavior Psychology

□ Fact/Introduction

Some childish acts done by adults are forgivable and even cute. But, some are tough and break the social rule.

□ Explanation/Body

Scientists said that Internet game is the key reason that bothers the mental growing of the grown-up person. Under the affection of the game type and the visual scene, adults' mood and creativities are largely affected. This result surely comes later. For example, adults showing continuous bothering the meeting and rude manner to other people are being affected by the Internet game. More and more adults are showing that they are still in the teenager condition.

□ Assertion/Conclusion

In result, too much of playing the Internet game has no advantages on the mental growing. More scientific discoveries also show that the gamma rays from the screen slow down the blood stream of the brain.

Absorb Vocabulary and Expressions

What can be used as a substitute of the word and phrase below?
Feel free to refer to the previous article.

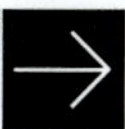

Example childish → **immature**

acts →

forgivable →

tough →

social rule →

said →

key reason →

grown-up person →

affection →

mood →

largely →

result →

surely →

comes →

bothering →

rude manner →

to →

teenager condition →

too much of playing →

advantages →

growing →

stream →

Create Your Own Sentence

-Make a sentence that contains the given word and phrase.
-Use the given words for any parts of speech such as a subject, verb, object, preposition object etc.
-You can change the form of the words.

1 immature behaviors

▸

2 excusable

▸

3 norm

▸

4 conclude

▸

5 emotions

▸

6. outcome

▸

7 continuous interrupting

▸

8 aggressive attitudes

▸

9 excessive playing

▸

10 circulation

▸

Rephrase the colored words and phrases

Change the colored words and expressions to more difficult and academic ones!
Knowing only one word for the writing will limit your skill, so you should have the alternatives.
This practice will lead you to the state-of-art academic and formal writing.

> **Excellent**

Young people from low class families often move directly from high school to adult world of work and being a parent.

>> **Impressive & Exceptional**

▸

> **Excellent**

Those from richer families, however, usually attend college and maybe graduate school,

>> **Impressive & Exceptional**

▸

> **Excellent**

continuing teenage years into the later twenties and even the thirties.

>> **Impressive & Exceptional**

▸

You can find more reading materials in this website and expand your knowledge for the rapidly changing world.

http://www.stresscure.com/hrn/addiction.html

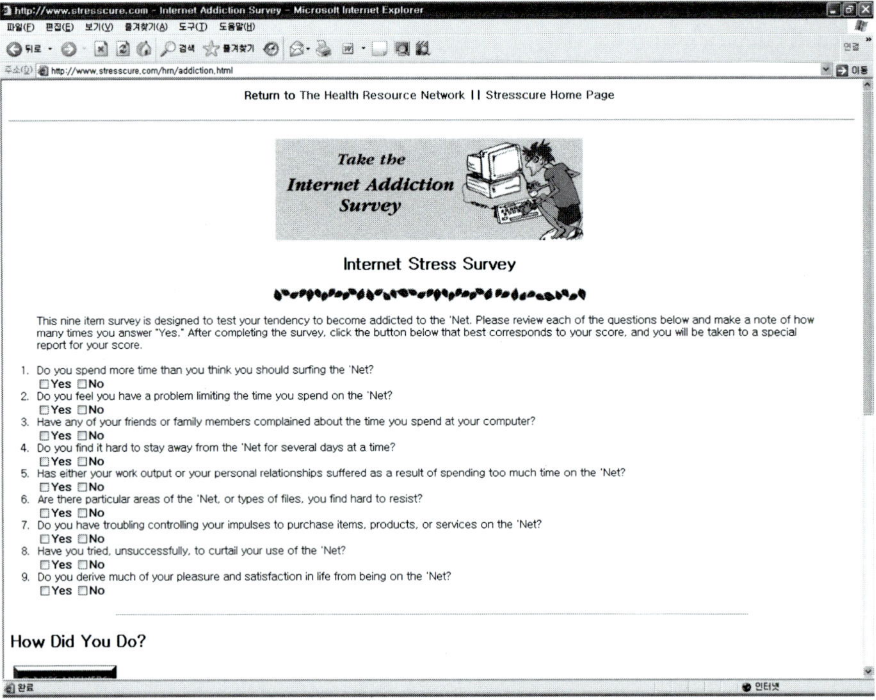

Return to The Health Resource Network || Stresscure Home Page

Take the Internet Addiction Survey

Internet Stress Survey

This nine item survey is designed to test your tendency to become addicted to the 'Net. Please review each of the questions below and make a note of how many times you answer "Yes." After completing the survey, click the button below that best corresponds to your score, and you will be taken to a special report for your score.

1. Do you spend more time than you think you should surfing the 'Net?
   ☐Yes ☐No
2. Do you feel you have a problem limiting the time you spend on the 'Net?
   ☐Yes ☐No
3. Have any of your friends or family members complained about the time you spend at your computer?
   ☐Yes ☐No
4. Do you find it hard to stay away from the 'Net for several days at a time?
   ☐Yes ☐No
5. Has either your work output or your personal relationships suffered as a result of spending too much time on the 'Net?
   ☐Yes ☐No
6. Are there particular areas of the 'Net, or types of files, you find hard to resist?
   ☐Yes ☐No
7. Do you have troubling controlling your impulses to purchase items, products, or services on the 'Net?
   ☐Yes ☐No
8. Have you tried, unsuccessfully, to curtail your use of the 'Net?
   ☐Yes ☐No
9. Do you derive much of your pleasure and satisfaction in life from being on the 'Net?
   ☐Yes ☐No

How Did You Do?

Level

Freshmen in University
TOEFL 6.0
1 year of studying in English speaking countries

Approximate word counts

129 words

Required Skill

Comfortable in using words like "turning the soil," "primitive," "vulnerable," "edible," "pasturage," "suitable," "livestock," "expanded," "domesticated," "animals," "collective living style," "rapid progress."

Target 10

Higher educational institutions and elite organizations require this level of writing!

The purpose of this practice is to have you experience the high level of writing and ready for the studying in a higher educational institution. You may find it extremely difficult in choosing right words and appropriate grammar while translating the given contents.
Consult "Vocabulary You Should Know!"

Title 사회의 변천
Course 역사

□ **Fact/Introduction**

농경시대에 농사기술은 제한되어 있었습니다. 사람들은 흙을 파서 엎고 땅에 물을 대어서 곡식을 재배했습니다.

□ **Explanation/Body**

이러한 초기의 방법은 자연의 힘에 매우 취약했습니다. 사람들은 급변하는 환경에 적응해야만 했습니다. 먹을 수 있는 식물을 기를 충분한 땅이 없어지면, 그들은 목축업으로 삶의 형태를 바꾸었습니다. 가축을 위한 적당한 자리를 찾기 위해서 한쪽에서 다른 쪽으로 이동함으로써 그들의 영역은 넓어졌습니다. 사회의 초기 형태는 사람들이 촌락을 세우면서 시작했습니다. 한자리에 오래 머무르기 위해서 그들은 쉽게 식량화할 수 있는 동물들을 계획적으로 길들였습니다.

□ **Assertion/Conclusion**

인간이 협동적인 삶의 형태를 갖춘 이후로, 사회는 급속히 성장했습니다. 작은 촌락들이 근대(近代)의 도시와 마을로 변화하는데 단지 몇 백 년 밖에 걸리지 않았습니다.

Vocabulary You Should Know!

The listed vocabulary follows the sequence of the content, not randomly mixed. This will help you find the appropriate vocabulary for your writing. Vocabulary here is not only helpful for the given writing but also leading you to the place where you are to be intelligent and educated. Remember that they are the suggestions. You can have your own choices of vocabulary for the writing which might be more acceptable than the suggested one.

- ▷ farming
- ▷ techniques
- ▷ Agricultural
- ▷ limited
- ▷ cultivated
- ▷ crops
- ▷ turning
- ▷ soil
- ▷ irrigating
- ▷ primitive
- ▷ vulnerable
- ▷ adapt
- ▷ rapidly
- ▷ circumstances
- ▷ enough land
- ▷ raise
- ▷ edible
- ▷ pasturage
- ▷ suitable
- ▷ livestock
- ▷ territories
- ▷ expanded
- ▷ form
- ▷ stay long
- ▷ deliberately
- ▷ domesticated
- ▷ accessible
- ▷ collective
- ▷ rapid
- ▷ reach

**Read the following article and compare with your writing.
As you read through, try to memorize the colored words and expressions.**

This is one of the translations for the given material. It is worth noting that many expressions used here are the professional level. Since you are assumed to write it in your own level, you should not blame yourself when you see differences between your writing and this article.

Title Transition of Society
Course History

□ **Fact/Introduction**

Farming techniques in the Agricultural Age were limited. People cultivated crops by turning the soil and irrigating the land.

□ **Explanation/Body**

These primitive ways were very vulnerable to the forces of nature. People had to adapt to the rapidly changing circumstances. When there was not enough land to raise edible plants, they changed their living pattern to the pasturage. By moving one place to another, searching for a suitable place for their livestock, their territories were expanded. The early form of society began as people built the village. In order to stay long in the same place, they deliberately domesticated animals for the easy accessible food.

□ **Assertion/Conclusion**

Since human beings formed the collective living style, the society makes rapid progress. It takes only a few hundred years to transform the small villages into the modern cities and towns.

Fill in the blank by using easier and simpler vocabulary and expressions you can think of.

Try to find easier vocabulary and expressions for the blank than you have written previously. You can see what is academic and what is casual. This practice enhances your memory of the words and its practicality. You can also have a clear understanding for the synonyms.

Title Transition of Society
Course History

□ **Fact/Introduction**

Farming ________ in the Agricultural _____ were ______. People ________ crops by ______ the soil and ________ the land.

□ **Explanation/Body**

These ________ ways were very _________ to the _____ of nature. People had to _____ to the ______ changing ___________. When there was not enough land to ____ ___________, they changed their living ______ to the ________. By moving one place to another, ________ for a _______ place for their ________, their ________ were _________. The early form of society began as people ____ the village. __________ stay long in _________ place, they __________ ___________ animals for the easy _________ food.

□ **Assertion/Conclusion**

Since human beings _______ the ______________ style, the society makes ____ _______. It takes only a few hundred years to ________ the small villages into the modern cities and towns.

Guide Article

Compare the vocabulary and phrases here with those you have used previously. Many students studying English say that they do not have much vocabulary. No! That is not true at all. The reason they feel this way is that they do not have enough experiences of substituting vocabulary and phrases for others. Vocabulary and phrases takes huge parts for your writing.

Title Transition of Society
Course History

□ **Fact/Introduction**

Farming [skills] in the Agricultural [Time] were [bad]. People [grew] crops by [tilling] the soil and [watering] the land.

□ **Explanation/Body**

These [old] ways were very [weak] to the [power] of nature. People had to [adjust] to the [quickly] changing [situation]. When there was not enough land to [grow] [plants that people could eat], they changed their living [style] to the [pastoral way of life]. By moving one place to another, [looking] for a [perfect] place for their [cattle], their [areas] were [extended]. The early form of society began as people [constructed/established] the village. [To] stay long in [one] place, they [carefully/purposely] [tamed] animals for the easy [reachable/handy] food.

□ **Assertion/Conclusion**

Since human beings [made] the [cooperative life] style, the society makes [quick] [development/growth]. It takes only a few hundred years to [turn] the small villages into the modern cities and towns.

Absorb Vocabulary and Expressions

What can be used as a substitute of the word and phrase below?
Feel free to refer to the previous article.

 **Example** skills → **techniques**

Agricultural Time →

bad →

People grew rice →

tilling →

watering →

old ways →

very weak →

the power of nature →

adjust →

quickly →

changing situation →

grow →

plants that people could eat →

pastoral way of life →

looking for →

perfect place →

cattle →

areas →

extended →

carefully →

tamed →

reachable/handy →

made →

cooperative life →

development/growth →

turn →

Create Your Own Sentence

-Make a sentence that contains the given word and phrase.
-Use the given words for any parts of speech such as a subject, verb, object, preposition object etc.
-You can change the form of the words.

1 agriculture

▸

2 irrigate

▸

3 vulnerable

▸

4 circumstances

▸

5 edible

▸

6. suitable

▸

7 territory

▸

8 expand

▸

9 domesticate

▸

10 collective

▸

Rephrase the colored words and phrases

Change the colored words and expressions to more difficult and academic ones!
Knowing only one word for the writing will limit your skill, so you should have the alternatives.
This practice will lead you to the state-of-art academic and formal writing.

> Excellent

While the growth of agrarian skills increase the scale of

>> Impressive & Exceptional

▶

> Excellent

human chances and helped city growth, it also made social life

>> Impressive & Exceptional

▶

> Excellent

more and more selfish and unfriendly.

>> Impressive & Exceptional

▶

You can find more reading materials in this website and expand your knowledge for the rapidly changing world.

http://indian-cultures.com

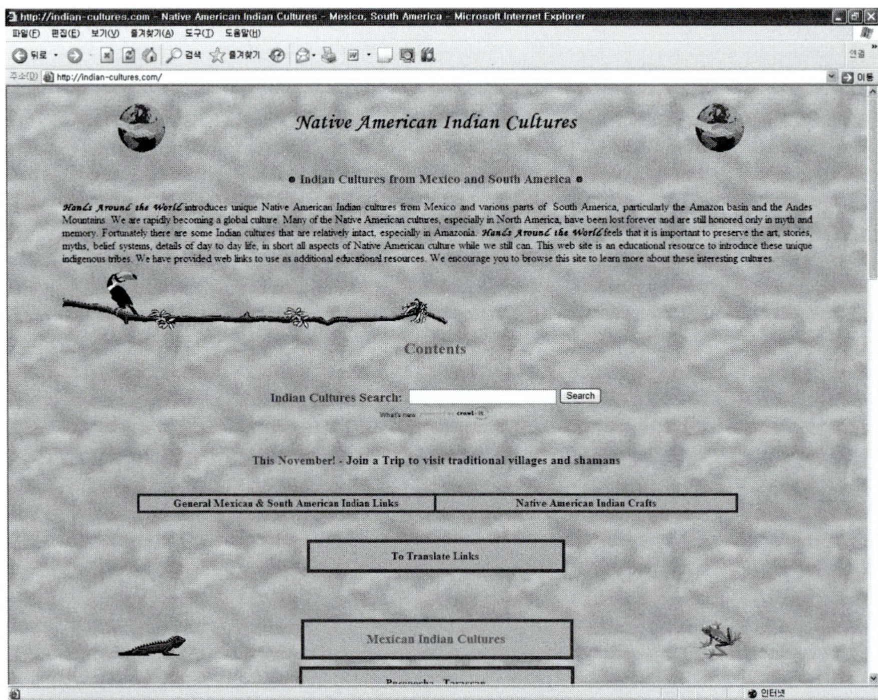

A sentence can be translated into various ways because each person has a different grammar level and a vocabulary skill. There should be an idea of appropriateness of the word usage and grammar application. However, it may not be wise to determine which sentence is linguistically right or wrong as long as a sentence you have created conveys the communicative message. Do not think that this Guideline is a concrete and fixed answer! What you have written may be better than the Guideline presented here.

Guideline

Target 01

Rephrase the colored words and phrases

The belief that one particular nation is superior to all others is a two-way street, of course. Just as we tend to dismiss those who differ from us, so others may judge us in the same way.

Target 02

Rephrase the colored words and phrases

A survey is a research method in which subjects respond to a series of statements or questions in a questionnaire or an interview.

Target 03

Rephrase the colored words and phrases

Consider the seemingly personal matter of deciding to change one's name, a practice especially common among celebrities in the United States. But are the names famous people use a matter of personal choice or are social forces at work?

Target 04

Rephrase the colored words and phrases

Our political system is based on the ideal of free choices just as we believe that our economy responds to the needs and choices of consumers.

Target 05

Rephrase the colored words and phrases

The students of the 1990s seem much more interested in being well off financially, while their counterparts in the late 1960s focused on developing a philosophy of life.

Target 06

Rephrase the colored words and phrases

Besides sharing patterns of living, people now participate in a global economy. Hundreds of independent economic systems, circumscribed by national borders, have been replaced by large corporations that manufacture and market goods throughout the world, and financial market, linked by satellite communication, operate around the clock.

Target 07

Rephrase the colored words and phrases

While a small number of people in the least-developed countries are rich, the majority confront the burden of surviving each day. These people live on the edge of survival not because of any personal short-coming, but because of the social organization of their societies.

Target 08

Rephrase the colored words and phrases

As skeleton, muscles, and various internal organs of the body each contribute to the survival of the human organism, Spencer maintained, so do machine structures.

Target 09

Rephrase the colored words and phrases

Young people from working-class families commonly move directly from high school to adult world of work and parenthood. Those from wealthier families, however, typically attend college and perhaps graduate school, extending adolescence into the later twenties and even the thirties.

Target 10

Rephrase the colored words and phrases

While the development of agrarian technology expanded the range of human opportunities and fueled urban growth, it also rendered social life more and more individualistic and impersonal.

TOP
LEVEL
WRITING
SENSE
THE ONE

For Elite Group

I

TOP
LEVEL
WRITING
SENSE
THE ONE
For Elite Group

I

TOP
LEVEL
WRITING
SENSE
THE ONE

For Elite Group

I